CONTENTS

Punta della Dogana
on the right,
at the end of
the Grand Canal.
On the other shore,
Piazza San Marco.
Behind the tip,
the baroque church
Santa Maria della Salute.
Beyond, the peninsula
of the Giudecca.
The first warehouses
date back to
the 18th century.

FRANÇOIS PINAULT, FROM ONE ISLAND TO THE NEXT, THE SAME PASSION

Jean-Jacques Aillagon was the French Minister of Culture and Communication from 2002 to 2004,
after being president of the Centre Georges Pompidou from 1996 to 2002. He ran Palazzo Grassi in 2006 and 2007.
He is now president of the Établissement Public du Musée et du Domaine National de Versailles.

JEAN-JACQUES AILLAGON RECOUNTS THE PINAULT ADVENTURE IN VENICE,
FROM THE PURCHASE OF PALAZZO GRASSI TO THAT OF PUNTA DELLA DOGANA.
A CHANCE FOR THE FORMER CULTURE MINISTER TO DWELL SOME OF THE CHARACTER
TRAITS OF THE MAN FROM BRITTANY, WHOSE DETERMINATION IS NOT THE LEAST
OF HIS QUALITIES.

Exactly four years ago, on May 10, 2005, François Pinault, in an exclusive article in *Le Monde*, announced his decision to abandon his project to create a museum for his collection on the Île Seguin at Boulogne-Billancourt and explained the reasons for his choice. His announcement provoked much speculation; certain individuals even implied that my advice was at the root of it. Knowing François Pinault as I do, these allegations never cease to amaze me: he knows how to listen, but when it comes to making a decision, he hears only himself, especially if the matter in question has to do with his business, his life, or his passion for art!

Some of the commentators also insinuated that François Pinault was giving up exhibiting his collection because he feared that it would be unable to withstand the scrutiny of public opinion. Naysayers also attributed his decision not to construct the building that Tadao Ando had designed for the Île Seguin to the fact that, owing to a downturn in business, he was unable to commit to such a heavy investment in a cultural institution.

The series of events that followed blatantly contradicted these interpretations, whose simple-mindedness directly reflected the ill-will on which they were founded. No later than May 13, François Pinault went to Venice to visit the newly elected mayor Massimo Cacciari, who had succeeded Paolo Costa, and to fix the conditions of sale of Palazzo Grassi. Palazzo Grassi had been owned and exploited by Fiat, in a brilliant fashion, until the death of Gianni Agnelli. Suffering from a number of unfavorable circumstances, from which it has since recovered, this important Italian company made known its desire to pull out of Palazzo Grassi. The mayor of Venice at the time, Paolo Costa, feared that this great cultural landmark would be converted, like so many others along the Grand Canal, into a hotel or company headquarters. It was he who, informed by Giandomenico Romanelli, director of museums in Venice and Pascaline Vatin, that I would be available upon leaving government office in April 2004, proposed that I create a cultural project for Grassi and become its director. First, however, the City had to resolve the question of the palace's pur-

6

chase from Fiat, keeping in mind that its temporary acquisition by the Casino of Venice, a company of public and private investors whose principal shareholder is the City of Venice, was only intended as an intermediary step, to ensure that the palace did not fall into the wrong hands. Knowing as I did the ins and outs of this prickly case, I suggested to François Pinault, as he began distancing himself from the Île Seguin, that he look more closely at Grassi, which was remarkably well-equipped in its time by Gae Alenti, is heir to an illustrious tradition, and is located in a major city that, furthermore, hosts the single most important international fine arts event. He reasoned quickly. He had known Gianni Agnelli well and was fully aware of the quality of the palace, which had already presented many large exhibitions. He made his decision promptly. His determination left no room for hesitation: shortly after acquiring Grassi, he entrusted its renovation to Tadao Ando, and scarcely six months later, in April 2006, the palace reopened with the exhibition "Where Are We Going? Works of the François Pinault Collection." On the very day of the acquisi-

tion of Grassi, Massimo Cacciari suggested, first jokingly then seriously, that François Pinault take an interest in the Dogana di Mare (Sea Customs House), a building in the form of the prow of a ship symbolizing Venice's maritime vocation. It had been abandoned for far too long and was on the verge of destruction. François Pinault replied, "Why not? We'll see." And see we did, quickly and well. When the City of Venice began looking for a contractor for the building, one who would be capable of generating and maintaining a center for contemporary art, François Pinault applied under the cover of Palazzo Grassi, which I was directing at the time. We came up against an unexpected rival, the Guggenheim. Competition was close and at times heated. Ultimately, the situation had the result of confirming François Pinault as a legitimate competitor to this prestigious institution, firmly anchored in 20th-century art, which its director Tom Krens had dragged into projects ranging from the exalting, to the uncertain, to the downright perilous. In the end, we won the day, which is how François Pinault found himself in the middle of a >

"Very early on,
François Pinault made
the choice to work
directly with the artists themselves
and often took the risk
of commissioning works."

second Venetian adventure, whose objective was to establish, between Palazzo Grassi and Punta della Dogana, a strong and permanent center of gravity for contemporary art.

The conclusion of this adventure provides the best possible answer to the critics of 2005. The Pinault collection does indeed exist. In Venice, Lille, and Moscow, it has shown itself to be one of the most brilliant in the world in the area of contemporary art. It is the reason why Punta della Dogana is able to meet such high expectations, though not in the way that a national institution would do. Rather than seeking to be "objectively comprehensive," it reflects individual choices and personal points of view that attest to a particular taste, sensibility, and passion.

Those who, in 2005, suspected that François Pinault was merely avoiding a heavy financial engagement have also been proven wrong by the choices made in Venice. The acquisition of Palazzo Grassi, its transformation by Tadao Ando, the financing of its activities for the past three years, the management of Punta della Dogana, its restoration, its renovation—again by Tadao Ando—, and the support given to its fledgling activities all illustrate the determination of the instigator of PPR to honor his commitments and see them through.

I have had the opportunity of participating in the François Pinault's move to and settlement in Venice. Working with him has allowed me to confirm what I already knew, or what I had sensed, about his personality. Determination plays an important role: it reveals the meaning of his project, his vision of what he must do, his ability to pursue the course he set for himself. It is, without a doubt, this character trait that most clearly reveals his roots in Brittany—an inland, farmland Brittany, the least pleasant, far from the delights of the coast, the most rustic and rugged, where farmers plow where they choose, in spite of doubts, worries, and

the nagging temptation to give up. This hardened endurance, which serves François Pinault in both his business and his private life, has nonetheless been tempered by more deliberately chosen—and even ardently desired—personality traits, in particular his interest, burgeoning into a passion, for the arts in general and contemporary art more specifically. Nothing in his heritage or upbringing had predisposed him to this love of the arts. As he often mentions, it is purely through the exercise of free will—or, in any case, by giving free rein to the vocation that had chosen him—that he was able, moving from the Pont-Aven School (a nod to Brittany), to Mondrian and Picasso, to Damien Hirst, to make art the central passion of his already very full life.

This chosen affinity goes far beyond the pleasure of knowing and owning works of art; it has brought them into the very heart of his existence as a collector and made them the driving force in the most intimate part of his life. François Pinault has often become attached, in an unusually radical way, to works that far surpass their function as pleasant or decorative objects. Very early on, he made the choice to work directly with the artists themselves and often took the risk of commissioning works. This process has, without a doubt, forged one of the most interesting aspects of François Pinault's relationship to art and one of the most singular characteristics of his collection. Is this not exactly what the opening exhibition at Punta della Dogana, created by Francesco Bonami and Alison Gingeras, attempts to demonstrate? This collaboration has also brought out other of François Pinault's good qualities: his sense of friendship, of loyalty, of indulgence coupled with terribly high expectations, and his ability (supposedly typically French; it was Descartes' rule of thumb) to avoid being lulled by insipid truths by constantly calling them into question.

•

ANONYMOUS
*Perspective Plan
of Venice*
Oil on wood.
Coll. musée du Louvre,
Paris.

PUNTA DELLA DOGANA IS ALREADY LITERATURE...

By **Dominique Muller** *is a French journalist and fiction writer.
Excerpt taken from "L'eau-delà de la pointe. À la Douane de Mer"*

10

**DOMINIQUE MULLER WRITES THRILLERS AND NOVELS. SHE LIKES
TO PENETRATE SECRETS. SHE JUST FINISHED A BOOK ON PUNTA DELLA DOGANA
THAT TELLS OF ITS HISTORY, ITS RENOVATION AND RENEWAL BY TADAO ANDO
AND ITS FUTURE IN THE HANDS OF FRANÇOIS PINAULT. DISCOVER AN EXCLUSIVE
EXCERPT FROM A TEXT THAT DESCRIBES A CUTTING-EDGE VENICE!**

"At the point where the waters of the Grand Canal and the broad Giudecca Canal meet, across from Saint Mark's Basin, appears the roof, like a row of overturned hulls, of Dogana di Mare, the Sea Custom House. What better place than this point, where the gaze encompasses the very idea of Venice, to erect such a sharp, jagged prow, demarcating without from within, exclusion from inclusion? Like those who settle their accounts in the hope of entering Paradise, or the Greek shades who paid to cross the Acheron on their path to the kingdom of Hades, those who wish to enter the city of Venice from the Adriatic Sea must also pay the price.

Dogana. The word comes from the Persian *diwàn*, meaning council of ministers and then, by extension, book of edicts. "A la porta, zoe chiamato in loro lenguazo al divan," noted the chronicler Marino Sanudo in his *Diarii* (Venice, 1529–1533). Imported from the East, from the Ottoman Empire and Byzantium, the Dogana was the keeper, in its warehouses, of whispered rumors from the Silk Road, of cargo from exotic ports, of the snap of sails and the creaking of masts. There was a custom house on land, near the Rialto Bridge, for merchandise arriving from the *terra firma*, familiar, common products, for everyday consumption. But Dogana di Mare was a different story altogether! It was the East come to the West, it was the far-off fortune of the Republic penetrating to its very heart, its nucleus, it was the concentration, in a single place, of the tangible, palpable, visible power of hard-working Venetians, the merchants and traders whose splendid palaces housed other warehouses and shops facing the canal through the broad entry to the Venetian Lagoon. The triangle of Dogana di Mare, its pure and simple design, captures the spirit of Venice in its glory days, a city of efficiency, organization, exchanges, and immense pride in work well-done. . . .

The Dogana is far from being a boastful, showy building, with the task of proclaiming the immense power of its city. It was constructed in order, like the Venetians, to do its job as a custom house, to welcome boats and to receive and stock merchandise, no more, no less. Its utilitarian function confers upon it the charm of the timid and introverted, the opposite of the brash, painted, >

dolled-up allure of a pin-up. If the Dogana were a woman, she would be a discreet and seemly beauty, bordering on the self-effacing, like those Alfred Hitchcock so admired for their ability to hide their stormy temper under a gray skirt-suit and button-up blouse. Maybe she would have the innocent features of Joan Fontaine as Mrs. de Winter, pitted against the seductive and diabolical ghost of Rebecca in a lavish castle, then happily spending the rest of her days with her tranquil husband. The story would be as follows: in 1682, the new Dogana di Mare, begun in 1677, moved to the point of sumptuous Venice, where it was cast in the shadow of the Basilica of Santa Maria della Salute, the church constructed by Baldassare Longhena to ward off the Black Plague and dedicated in 1687 after fifty years of construction. The little Dogana, whose figure of Fortune rises to barely 28 meters (92 feet), appears self-conscious beside the prestigious dome of its neighbor, celebrated each year by all of Venice. But she became so necessary, she so conscientiously applied herself to her task and maintained her rank that the Serenissima came to love her, so much that it has made her tip the emblem of the city. . . .

The tower that crowns it, situated at the convergence of the waterways, is a watchtower and a landmark for this liquid doorway to the city.

A competition was announced in 1676, in which several celebrated architects, including Longhena, participated.

Giuseppe Benoni was chosen as the winner in 1677. He was not only an architect, but also a hydraulic engineer associated with the Magistrate of Waterworks. Thanks to his capabilities, so useful at this site—actually almost a non-site—the city assumed responsibility for the project and the construction of the new Punta della Dogana, Dogana di Mare. He gave his building, designed and built following the footprint and volumes of the previous structure, such a broad, limpid, floor plan that, even throughout successive generations of customs officials and renovations, its fundamental structure remained unchanged.

Using wooden posts, stone, and brick, Benoni managed to strike the right note, a harmonious chord that resolved the contradiction between the linear flatness of time and space, the here and now, and the longing for departure, to "escape, escape far away," the questioning of the horizon suggested by the point. . . .

Punta della Dogana is a thought in stone that evokes, in whomever contemplates it and from whatever angle, the certainty that each person has his place in the world, that it is possible to discover this place, and that, once it has been found, life will become as simple, evident, and serene as the triangle of the Dogana. Benoni designed a building intended for work, commerce, and the circulation of goods and money. Unlike most Venetian symbols of power, pleasure, or faith, its walls are nearly devoid of superfluous ornamentation, statues, allegories, and figures, with the exception of the empty-eyed horse heads situated under the overhang of the tower, and the high-relief lion heads that decorate the keystones. One of the lions, with a full, curly mane, symbolizes Saint Mark. Holding the Book between his paws, he directs his gaze toward the Piazza San Marco, on the other side of the Basin. A long, thin border of volutes, imitating the waves of the waterway, runs along the underside of the cornice of the façade.

Alone at the tip of the point, the summit of the small square tower denotes the vastness of the world. Two bronze atlantes support a golden globe topped with the figure of Fortune, who holds a shield—or maybe it is a scythe in the shape of a crescent moon—and turns into the wind. These few elements of modest size, respectful of a certain sobriety and economy of means, capture the mythology of coincidence, chance, and destiny that preside over the world. **>**

PUNTA DELLA DOGANA
IN A FEW DATES

15TH CENTURY
Building of the first warehouses
on the Punta.

1418
Creation of the first Dogana di Mare.

1631–1687
Construction of the church Santa
Maria della Salute by Baldassare
Longhena.

1677–1682
Construction of the new Dogana di
Mare, designed by Giuseppe Benoni.

1835
Giovanni Alvise Pigozzi restores the
building and modifies it.

APRIL 27, 2007
Palazzo Grassi wins
the competition for the creation
of a contemporary art center
at Punta della Dogana.

SEPTEMBER 20, 2007
Presentation of the model
by François Pinault, Tadao Ando
and Massimo Cacciari.

JANUARY 2008–MARCH 2009
Fourteen months of restoration
work.

JUNE 6, 2009
Opening of the exhibition "Mapping
the Studio—Artists from the François
Pinault Collection."

Fortune, sculpted by Bernardo Falconi, also implies "tempest," as in the *fortuna maris*, or "peril of the sea" in Latin. The "means of fortune," *mezza di fortuna*, designated the small boats that brought passengers to and from a ship anchored in a harbor or port. Peril of the sea is the term given in admiralty law to all unforeseeable risks for which the shipowner must account and against which he protects himself in contracts through a "bad luck" clause. This young woman, who covers the world with her shield and turns into the winds of the point, is also a marine goddess, a savior and protectress of the seafarer and his ship in times of storm.

Her duty in the world, at the tip of Punta della Dogana, is to ensure the customs operations; she is a Venetian at work for whom the sun continues to rise, as it did for the Pharaoh's Egyptians. To accomplish its task, the building is outfitted with nine bays, each ten meters wide and seven meters from floor to beams, with one door leading from the Giudecca Canal, where the goods arrive, and another to the Grand Canal, where the goods leave after passing

through the warehouse. . . .

Since the beginning of the 1990s, the ships entering through the Porto di Lido see the Dogana as they pass but no longer stop. Too big, too long, too tall, in fact bigger, longer, and taller than the dilapidated building, with its disjointed stones, it now houses only a few offices. Dogana di Mare, like Venice itself, is old, diseased, suffering from the ills of old age. But while the city hides its condition under a façade of coquetry, preening, make-up, and cross-dressing, presided over by commercial billboards, the point, timid and reserved, expires slowly, quietly, and inexorably. At the very end of the 20th century, the point was closed for security reasons: it is now impossible to stroll by the Dogana or to pass from the Grand Canal to the Giudecca Canal in a few steps. Becoming damaged, cracked, wrinkled, deformed, perishing: such is the fate of the very old, not only of humans, but also of stones.

But Fortune remains, on high, and refuses to be disarmed. Punta della Dogana, the watchtower of the lagoon, between the sea and dry land, the perfect compromise between near and far, cannot become the

THREE QUESTIONS
FOR RENATA CODELLO,
the superintendent of Venice

HOW IMPORTANT IS THE CONSERVATION OF A BUILDING LIKE PUNTA DELLA DOGANA FOR THE CITY OF VENICE AND FOR ITS ARTISTIC HERITAGE?

The conservation of Punta della Dogana and its transformation
into a center for contemporary art are of the utmost importance.
While the exterior is characterized by monumental façades,
the interior has undergone serious modifications,
due in particular to the division of the historical docks of
Punta della Dogana. It had become urgent to intervene in order
to save the historical architecture, but that was only possible
on the condition of finding a new function for the space that could
make use of and highlight the beauty of the large
17th century rooms. The operation was in any case quite
complicated, and the final result presented to the visitors
is the outcome of outstanding teamwork.

WHAT MOTIVATED THE CITY'S CHOICE TO ENTRUST THIS PIECE OF ITS HERITAGE TO THE FRANÇOIS PINAULT FOUNDATION—AND THEREFORE TO TADAO ANDO—AND TO USE IT AS AN EXHIBITION SITE FOR CONTEMPORARY ART?

The Pinault project was selected following a competition
organized by the City of Venice. Tadao Ando's work has revealed
itself to be in perfect harmony with both the history of the custom
house and with its new use as a center for contemporary art.
It has established a wonderful link between the past and
the future, and the interiors are now all the more meaningful.

WHAT PLACE DOES PUNTA DELLA DOGANA OCCUPY IN THE CULTURAL POLITICS OF VENICE?

Even the greatest skeptics now admit that it was worth facing
the challenge of restoring Punta della Dogana. The mayor Massimo
Cacciari, François Pinault and the superintendency of Venice
believed in the success of the project and worked hard to make it
come true. Today, Venice benefits from a new site for contemporary
art, which reinforces the activities of the Biennale and of other
foundations. The result, which demonstrates the huge potential
of this city, bodes well for the future.

Tadao Ando was the
1995 Pritzker Prize
laureate. Collaboration
between the architect
and François Pinault
began in 2001.

TADAO ANDO OR THE SPIRIT OF PLACE

Philip Jodidio, *author of about sixty books on contemporary architecture, including "Ando Complete Works" (Taschen, 2006).*

16

**BY MAKING CONSTANT REFERENCE TO THE CONCEPT OF
GENIUS LOCI ("THE SPIRIT OF PLACE") AS A FOUNDING ENERGY
FOR HIS THOUGHT, TADAO ANDO HAS ACHIEVED
A VERY SUBTLE AND PURE REHABILITATION OF PUNTA
DELLA DOGANA. A VENETIAN RENAISSANCE THAT OWES A LOT
TO HIS BOND WITH FRANÇOIS PINAULT.**

Tadao Ando, born in Osaka in 1941, was a self-taught architect. He founded Tadao Ando Architect & Associates in Osaka in 1969 and won the 1995 Pritzker Prize, often compared to the Nobel for architecture. Ando's work, which frequently incorporates concrete, is characterized by the use of basic geometric forms such as circles or rectangles. Especially in Japan, where construction methods allow for very high quality, Ando's concrete has a silken, refined presence in spite of its mass, which places his work in a category of its own. Clearly one of the most notable and influential architects working today, Ando has extensive experience in the area of museum design and is known for his ability to adapt his designs to the constraints of sites.

The working relationship between the architect and François Pinault began in 2001 when Tadao Ando was selected in an international competition to build the Fondation d'Art Contemporain Francois Pinault, on the Île Seguin on the Seine River near Paris. Though not graced with 17th-century architecture, the site was located at the tip of the island, the setting of a legendary **>**

LEFT
Symbol of Punta
della Dogana,
sketch by Tadao Ando.

RIGHT
Cross-section of
the central courtyard
of Punta della Dogana,
East side (up)
and West side (down),
November 2007.

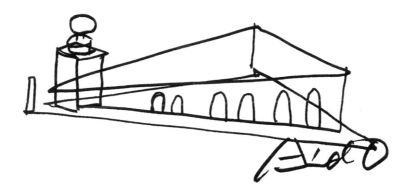

18

automobile plant. "The power of France is the power of culture," said Tadao Ando at the time. "The Seine has been the lifeline of culture, linking the cultural monuments of Paris. This island also has a history as a stronghold of industry, having once been the site of a Renault plant." The sensitivity he showed in Paris to the industrial history of the Ile Seguin is one of the reasons of his later affinities with the same client in Venice.

For reasons related to local bureaucracy, François Pinault decided not to pursue the Île Seguin project and set his sights instead on Venice. He commissioned Tadao Ando to renovate the 18th-century Palazzo Grassi on the Grand Canal in Venice. The building had been used by Fiat to organize exhibitions for more than twenty years and was renovated in 1983 by the Italian designer Gae Aulenti. Historic preservation guidelines required that neither the façades nor significant interior details be modified. Tadao Ando thus faced the challenge of creating appropriate spaces for the exhibition of very contemporary art within old walls. He carried out the project between September 2005 and April 2006. "We

ANDO MUSEUMS WORLDWIDE

Tadao Ando's recent museums include the Modern Art Museum of Fort Worth (Fort Worth, Texas, US, 1999–2002); the Pulitzer Foundation for the Arts (Saint-Louis, Missouri, US, 1997–2000), the Chichu Art Museum on the Island of Naoshima in the Inland Sea of Japan (2002–2004), and, more recently, the Clark Art and Conservation Center (Stone Hill Center, Williamstown, Massachusetts, US, 2006–2008). He is presently working on the Abu Dhabi Maritime Museum (Abu Dhabi, UAE, begun in 2006), which will neighbor Jean Nouvel's Louvre building on Saadiyat Island.

studied plan layouts with nested exhibition spaces enclosed by white walls," explains the architect. "At that point, we were not concerned with creating a self-contained white-cube exhibition space but focused more on investigating details that would take advantage of the spatial essence of the existing building surrounding them... In spaces that intentionally evoke surprise and discovery, art seems to abruptly appear, following a spatial sequence that encourages a dialogue between old and new."

This was not the first building to be renovated by Tadao Ando. He had restored and enlarged the International Library of Children's Literature (Tokyo, Japan, 1997–2002) in the old Ueno Library built in 1906, giving the original, incomplete design a coherence it had always lacked. Italian designer Giorgio Armani asked Tadao Ando to renovate a former Nestle factory on the Via Borgognone in Milan. Leaving the existing structure largely in place, the architect inserted a "theater" for fashion, as well as a showroom and offices, into the building. His Teatro Armani in Milan (1999–2002) is a study in the willful contrast of the (industrial) old and the (fashionable) new.

Though it is prestigious and well located, Palazzo Grassi's exhibition space is limited, and François Pinault saw the need to create another location for his collection of contemporary art. The Guggenheim Foundation, associated with the architect Zaha Hadid, made a bid to install its own collections in the Punta della Dogana building, but the city opted for the plan put forth by François Pinault, again associated with Tadao Ando. Design work on the structure began in May 2007 and the inauguration took place in June 2009. Though older than Palazzo Grassi, the Dogana presented a similar challenge. "Just as with Palazzo Grassi," says Tadao Ando, "for the exterior as well as the interior, any alterations other than a return to the original appearance are severely restricted according to the laws concerning the preservation >

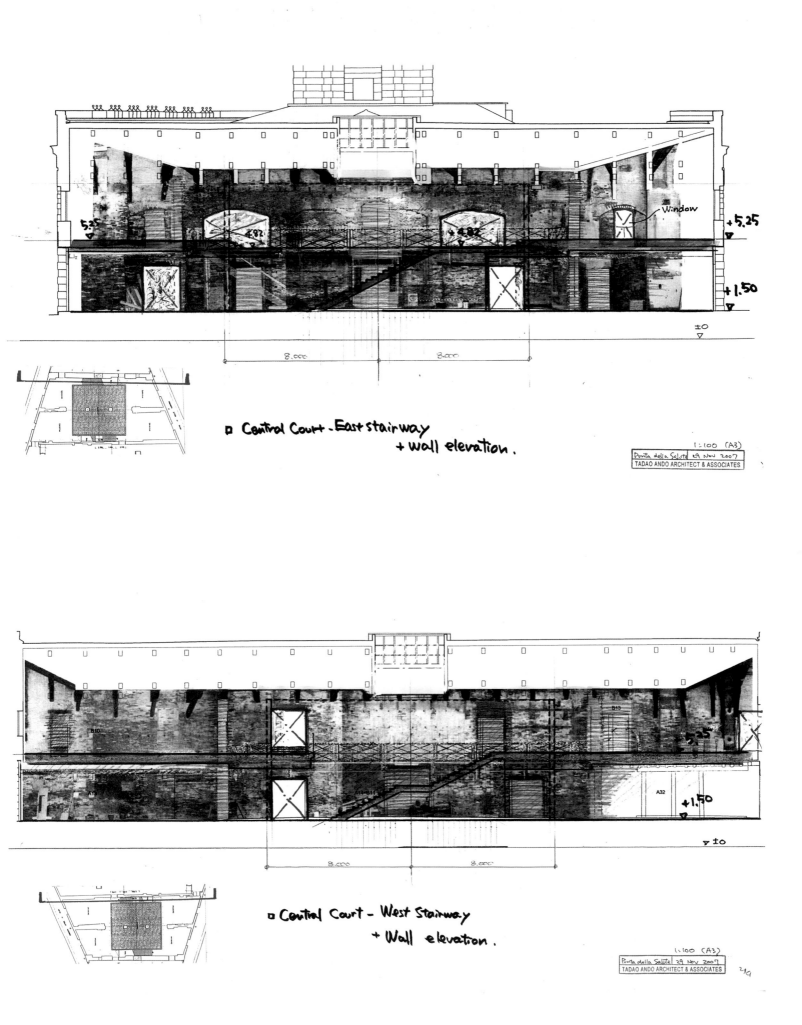

□ Central Court - East stairway
         + wall elevation.

+5.25

+1.50

Window

5.25

+4.82

±0

8.000   8.000

1:100 (A3)
Punta della Salute 29 Nov 2007
TADAO ANDO ARCHITECT & ASSOCIATES

□ Central Court - West Stairway
         + Wall elevation.

+1.50

5.25

±0

8.000   8.000

1:100 (A3)
Punta della Salute 29 Nov 2007
TADAO ANDO ARCHITECT & ASSOCIATES

Punta della Dogana
model.

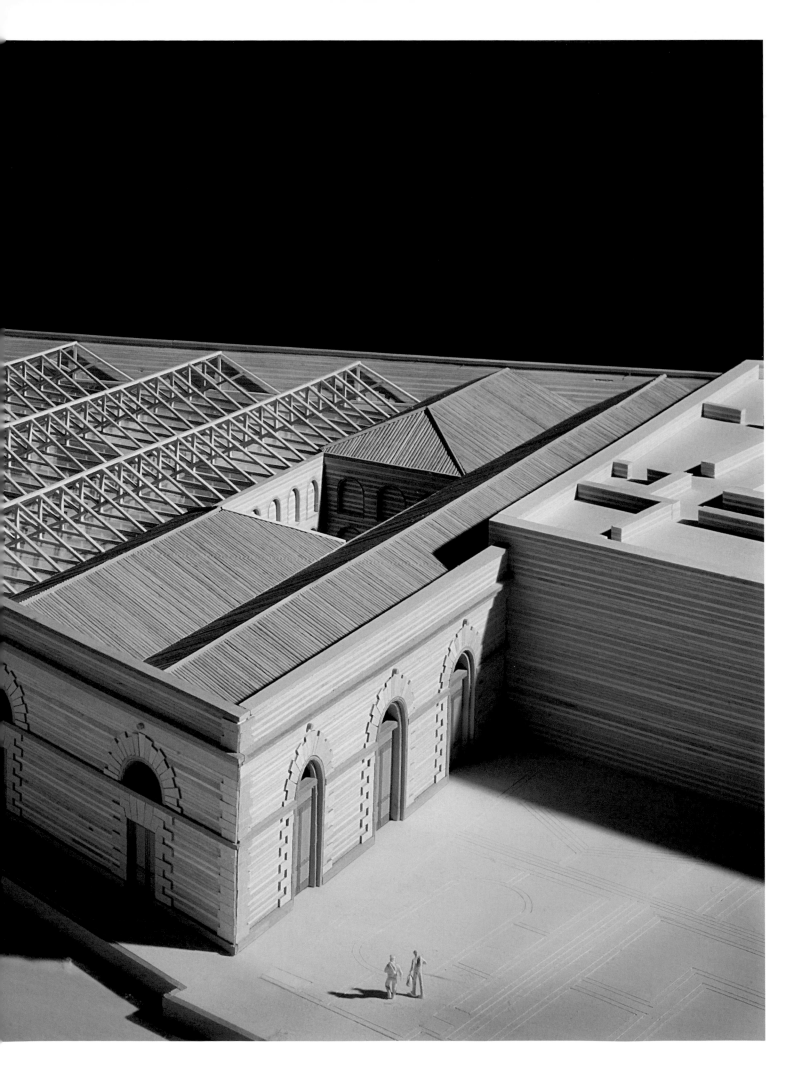

of historical structures. Within these constraints, we were again faced with the theme of how to produce a modern space while drawing out the latent power of the original building. By exposing the bricks of hidden walls and the wooden roof trusses that had been concealed during the frequent renovations, I wanted to further emphasize the charm of the spaces by adding just a few new architectural elements, while manifesting the individuality of the building."

OLD MEETS NEW

Tellingly, Ando has chosen to see the architecture in terms of its basic, geometric form. He says, "The Punta della Dogana building is characterized by a simple, rational structure. The volume creates a triangle, a direct reference to the shape of the tip of the island of Dorsoduro, while the interiors are divided into long rectangles, with a series of parallel walls." Though he paid a great deal of attention to the renovation of the existing structure, Tadao Ando did allow himself one powerful act of geometry in the middle of the triangular layout of the building—a concrete cube that rises to the full height of the structure and becomes the axis of all paths leading through the renovated space. Ando also designed twenty metal gates for the water entrances of the building, in a nod to the work of another modern architect who also pitted himself against the ancient stones of Venice—Carlo Scarpa, in his Olivetti Showroom on Saint Mark's Square (1957).

In both Palazzo Grassi and Punta della Dogana, Ando was faced with the problem of preserving the existing monument while readying it for the exhibition of contemporary art. He states, "The plan of the Palazzo Grassi project was to renovate a building from the late 18th century and convert it into a contemporary art museum, where I was requested by Mr. Pinault to do minimal refurbishment. In accordance with stringent restrictions, I removed decorations

that had been added during previous renovations to recover the original design by Giorgio Massari and added a minimum of new elements. In this project, I pursued the theme of the encounter and clash between old and new (historical architecture and contemporary art)." Visitors to Palazzo Grassi might indeed be forgiven if they do not always spot the strong modernity that usually marks the style of Ando. "In the Palazzo Grassi renovation," he goes on to say, "I tried to create a new world within the limits of the framework of the existing building, by paring the building down to its original state and enhancing the space with a just a few elements. In the Punta della Dogana renovation, on the other hand, I had, to some extent, greater flexibility to design new spaces. I intended to provoke a dramatic clash between old and new by inserting a space bounded by concrete walls inside the existing structure; such an exercise reveals the various historical layers, bringing along a sense of clarity and understanding, instead of covering or destroying history."

THE SIMPLICITY OF PERFECTION

Tadao Ando is nonetheless best known for the buildings he has designed entirely. The real question is why François Pinault, a knowledgeable and passionate collector of contemporary art, would ask such an architect to work within a historical building instead of creating a new structure like that originally designed for the Île Seguin. "I have known Tadao Ando and his architecture for many years," states François Pinault. "We decided together to build a museum and it was the occasion for us to work together quite intensively. With the simple geometric forms of his concrete buildings, Ando is one of a line of architects whose thought has inspired and nourished contemporary construction. He seeks to find a new path, born of the fusion of the wealth of Japanese traditions with modern Western society, ▸

□ Exibition Area 1

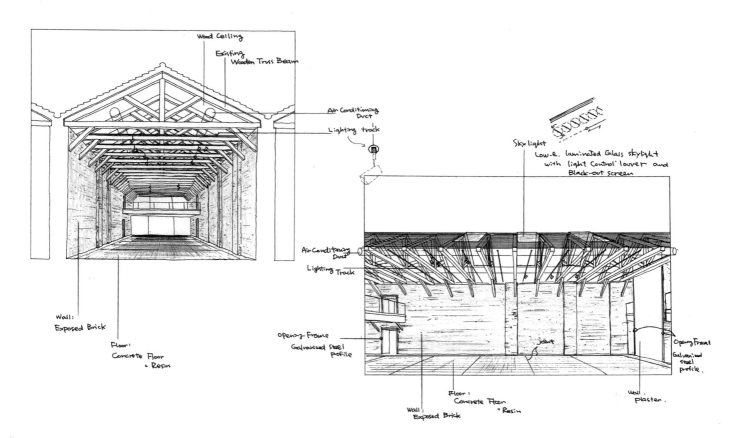

Wood Ceiling

Existing Wooden Truss Beam

Air Conditioning Duct

Lighting track

Skylight
Low-e. laminated Glass skylight with light Control louver and Black-out screen

Air Conditioning Duct

Lighting Track

Wall:
Exposed Brick

Floor:
Concrete Floor + Resin

Opening Frame
Galvanized steel profile

Opening Frame
Galvanized steel profile.

Joint

Floor:
Concrete Floor + Resin

Wall:
Exposed Brick

Wall.
plaster.

□ Exhibition Area 2 (Central Gallery)

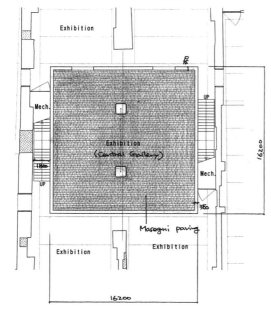

Exhibition

Mech.

UP

Exhibition
(Central Gallery)

16200

Mech.

UP

Masegni paving

Exhibition

Exhibition

16200

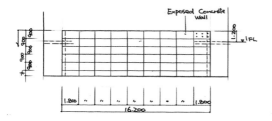

Exposed Concrete Wall

1FL

1800   1800
16200

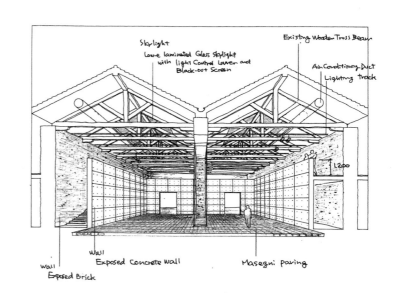

Skylight
Low-e laminated Glass skylight with light Control louver and Black-out Screen

Existing Wooden Truss Beam

Air Conditioning Duct

Lighting track

1200

Wall
Exposed Brick

Wall
Exposed Concrete Wall

Masegni paving

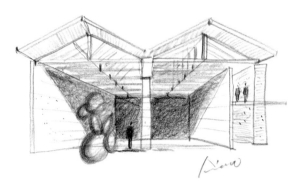

24

a path that reconciles the individual and the environment. In Venice, the challenge was to create a place for the exhibition of contemporary art, while conserving the essence of a building so full of memory and history. The choice of Tadao Ando to carry out this project seemed quite obvious to me. He is one of the rare architects who knows how to step back and allow nature, or the urban context of a building, to bring about the creation, or in this instance, the resuscitation of a masterpiece. Both at Palazzo Grassi and at Punta della Dogana, he has efficiently and subtly carried out renovations that give the impression that these buildings were, from the first, destined to exhibit works of art."

Ultimately, the success of Tadao Ando's Punta della Dogana will depend on how visitors experience the art that is on display, how they react to the building, and how it ages with time. In appraising the project, François Pinault himself insists on its enduring qualities. "At Punta della Dogana, Tadao Ando opted for a radical approach," he says. "He imagined architectural forms that are at once imperious and fragile, spectacular yet discreet, just as they are simultaneously respectful and audacious. The exterior of the building has been restored, while the interior was literally recreated with galleries that inhabit this exceptional building both in spirit and in form. The spaces conceived by Tadao Ando are both coherent and varied in their configuration, creating singular moods, that range from unexpected to calm and minimal, as is the case in the central cube that occupies the very heart of the museum. Here again, Tadao Ando succeeded brilliantly in reconciling visual perfection with the most complete simplicity, creating a timeless universe." Though the contemporary art shown within its walls may change over time, Punta della Dogana has entered the 21st century thanks to the vision and commitment of François Pinault and Tadao Ando. Here, at least, the city is more than the shadow of its former glory.

•

THE STORY OF AN EXCEPTIONAL BUILDING SITE

Marc Desportes, *foreman of the Punta della Dogana project,*
representative of the contractor.

26

**IT WAS A CHALLENGE TO TIME, TO HISTORY, TO THE FUTURE,
IT WAS MOST OF ALL A HUMAN ADVENTURE WHERE
120 WORKERS STRIVED DAY IN AND DAY OUT FOR FOURTEEN
MONTHS, WHERE AN EPHEMERAL PORT WAS BUILT AND
WHERE 16TH CENTURY BRICKS WERE BROUGHT TO LIGHT.**

From a contractor's point of view, the renovation of Punta della Dogana was remarkable for three reasons: time—the work was done in only fourteen months—, quality—it incorporates both traditional Venetian craftsmanship and state-of-the-art technology—, and cost—the budget of 20 million euros initially slated for the project was respected.

As soon as Palazzo Grassi was chosen to spearhead the project for a center for contemporary art at Punta della Dogana, in June 2007, we established a feasible plan with Jean-Jacques Aillagon, who was still the director of Palazzo Grassi at the time, and ordered the architectural studies to be done during the summer so we could present the project to the press on September 19, 2007. In the fall, agreements were reached with the various subcontractors, many of whom had already worked on the renovation of Palazzo Grassi from May 2005 to April 2006. Their having already collaborated with Tadao Ando and the same group of local engineers and architects, led by Eugenio Tranquilli, helped make discussion and decision-making run smoothly. We also >

"A temporary port created at the point served as our lifeline to dry land."

immediately undertook all of the preparatory work, the "undressing" of the building by demolishing non-structural elements, to gain time and to be ready to begin the actual renovation as soon as the various permits and administrative authorizations were obtained. Construction began in earnest in mid-January 2008 and was completed in March 2009.

The construction site was meticulously organized and remarkably led by the Dottor company: we had to make space in a very limited surface area for the storage of a minimum of materials, for the living quarters of the workers, for circulating on the work site, and of course for construction itself. A temporary port created at the point served as our lifeline to dry land: everything passed through there, including soil, gravel, portable buildings, materials, cranes, machines... The most impressive, without a doubt, were the cement mixers, which arrived, complete with their pumps, on huge barges.

Renovating a building means discovering it. Punta della Dogana has a long history stretching back to its creation in the 17th century. It had already been restored by the Austrians in 1830–1840, then had been put to various uses throughout the 20th century. As a result, each time we discovered a new element, we had to determine, with the superintendent of historical monuments of Venice, Tadao Ando, and François Pinault, the relevance of maintaining the element, or the possibility of discarding it if it infringed upon the architectural project. We were thus able to obtain authorization to remove the cement slab floor on the second level that dated from the 1950s, which enabled us to both reestablish the building in its original condition and have as many two-storey rooms as possible.

Punta della Dogana is an exceptional place that rejects the artificial. If you try to incorporate anything that is the least bit inau-

thentic, it is immediately visible. As a case in point, we had to occasionally build false fronts in brick to mask parts of the existing wall that were too damaged to display but that we could not eliminate. These new parts of the wall are extremely visible. The place itself has such a presence that it rejects pastiche. On the other hand, it has incorporated Tadao Ando's architectonic cement modules marvelously: the two elements communicate with and enhance one another.   •

THE BUILDING SITE OF PUNTA DELLA DOGANA IN FIGURES

5,000 M² of surface area
210 METERS of facade on the canals
75 METERS of facade on the Campo della Salute
20 monumental glass and steel **DOORS**
9 NAVES of an average width of 10 meters and an internal height of 7 meters
28 METERS in height for the tower crowned by *la Fortuna*
5,000 M² of restored walls made with reused bricks
130 WOODEN TRUSSES for the roof structure
90,000 TILES laid on the roof
10,000 TONS of various transported materials
2,000 VOYAGES between the construction site and the mainland
120 CONSTRUCTION WORKERS for 300,000 work hours
Total budget of **20 MILLION EUROS**

Before its restauration, Punta della Dogana showed 58 openings. Today, their number has been reduced to 18 so the visitor can circulate from one navata to the other.

THREE QUESTIONS
FOR EUGENIO TRANQUILLI
General coordinator for the restoration

HOW DID TADAO ANDO'S PROJECT FIT INTO A HISTORICAL BUILDING AS UNUSUAL AS PUNTA DELLA DOGANA?
After first visiting the building, Tadao Ando thought of intervening only minimally, to open up as many exhibition spaces as possible and allow monumental works to be installed. The interior of the building had undergone major changes over the course of the 20th century: walls had been constructed, mezzanine floors and passages created... Tadao Ando wished to eliminate all of the "modern" additions and restore the original layout of the building, in particular the two-storey central courtyard dating back to the 17th century, the "cortile" that is a typical part of Venetian palaces, including Palazzo Grassi. The brick columns attest to the thickness of the walls, designed to resist the pressure of the loose grains stored in the warehouses on the ground floor. Inside the courtyard, Tadao Ando proposed to create four walls out of the refined cement that is such a signature element of his work and which would remain separate from the historical structure. Taking into account the autonomy of this construction, the committee for the conservation of Venice accepted, considering in fact that it was a contemporary creation comparable to the pieces slated to be exhibited at Punta della Dogana. Looking carefully at the building today, one notices that there is always a narrow space between the original walls and the concrete and glass constructions by Tadao Ando, which makes the exciting juxtaposition of two strong architectural types all the more apparent. **>**

The height of
the concrete walls and
their openings were
designed to allow
an overall reading
of the two navatas.

ON THE OUTSIDE, THE WOVEN STEEL GATES SUBTLY SIGNAL THE NEW IDENTITY OF PUNTA DELLA DOGANA...

For the façades, Tadao Ando first wanted to restore what originally existed, without making any additions, and recreate the traditional Venetian wooden doors. But Massimo Cacciari, the mayor of Venise, insisted that the architect's strong presence on the inside also be visible from the outside, a sign of Venice's "reawakening." We therefore transformed all of the exterior windows and doors. The difficulty in Venice, however, is that the window glass must not generate reflections that might hinder the maneuvering of the boats in the Laguna. Tadao Ando chose to reference the work of Carlo Scarpa who is, with Palladio, one of the architects he most admires, by taking up the idea of the woven steel gates used by Scarpa at the Olivetti showroom in San Marco and placing them in front of the glass doors and windows of Punta della Dogana.

HOW DID YOU RESOLVE THE QUESTION OF LIGHTING THE WORKS?

The storage rooms had to be protected against water and thieves. Therefore, the only light came from the windows of the offices and the skylights. Because natural light was lacking, we installed an extremely flexible lighting system that uses the roof trusses as a support. Two parallel tubes run the length of the walls. The first diffuses a light that "washes" the surface of the wall, while the second is for installing spotlights, depending on the works of art. There is also a third line provides basic lighting, which is inserted in the gutters of the trusses. These same gutters hold the air conditioning, the electricity, and the computer and security systems.

THE PROTECTIVE SHELL

At the same time as the installation of small pilings in the floor
to stabilize the anchoring of the building—in particular at the tip—,
a protective shell to prevent flooding was added in the spring
of 2008. It was probably the most difficult phase of the renovation
because the construction workers had to labor in the mud,
sometimes with water almost up to their waist. It was also the most
delicate phase because the protection against the water needed
to be perfect. If there were the smallest flaw, water would enter into
the conduits designed to hold the technological systems and the
museum would be susceptible to flooding at the first *Alta Aqua*. The
shell is constituted, in fact, of a layer that covers the entire surface
of the building, with waterproofing in the walls up to a height of
2.10 meters. Between two thin concrete layers, a sheath prevents
water seepage. Because it was impossible to work in the basement
—the displacement of fine sediment would likely have destabilized
the building— or to puncture the walls designed to contain
the infrastructure systems (electricity, ventilation, heating...),
conduits designed to hold the technological systems were set up
within the shell itself. It was thus necessary to position the various
infrastructure systems required for the functioning of the museum
well in advance. Construction was preceded by preventive
archaeological excavations that mainly revealed a succession of
building foundations dating back to the 16th century, a time when it
was still a somewhat marshy area cleared for the city. As expected,
nothing was found. The 16th-century layer, with its bricks placed on
the ground, was magnificent to see: the bricks, conforming
to the earth, had adopted the shape of the ground. M.D.

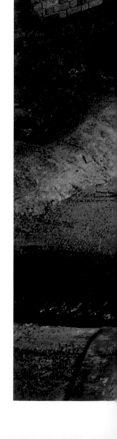

ABOVE

Preventive
archaeological
excavations have
revealed a succession
of ground layers.
On the 16th-century
layer, the bricks have
adopted the shape
of the ground.

RIGHT

A concrete protective
shell against flooding
covers the entire surface
of the building.

THE BRICKS

In order to renovate all of the masonry elements, the traditional
technique of *scuci-cuci* (remove/replace) is used in Venice
in order to prevent the absorption of the salt and water
into the walls, already coated with *marmorino* that absorbs salt
before being "sacrificed" and replaced every two or three years.
The Venetian *muratori* (wall makers) removed, one by one,
the old bricks "eaten" by sea water and replaced them with other
old bricks, in good condition. These bricks are reclaimed bricks
bought on the mainland and selected according to their size, color,
and shape. Depending on their hue and dimensions,
one can deduce the firing technique and therefore the time period.
The *savoir-faire* of the *muratori* in choosing these bricks,
and in deciding on a mortar or a coating, is essential for
the coherence of the renovation. It has not changed
since the original construction of Punta della Dogana an is
reminiscent of the Japanese architectural tradition
according to which the building's original construction method is
more important than the building itself. The difficulty with
this meticulous work is in knowing where to do it and when
to stop In order to achieve the right balance between the required
intervention, the desired intervention and no intervention.
Certain walls that appear damaged but remain structurally sound
have in this way been preserved because they testify
to the strength of the building. M.D.

150,000 bricks were
found in the 16th and
17th-century buildings.
The ancestral *savoir-faire*
of the Venitian *muratori*
[wall makers] is essential
for the coherence of the
renovation. It is similar to
Japanese architectural
tradition according
to which the building's
original construction
method is more important
than the building itself.

THE CONCRETE

All the concrete employed by Tadao Ando is exceptional.
It possesses unique qualities: very smooth, light gray, with
evenly spaced joints produced by the concrete formwork,
yet with some small imperfections that testify to the
unpredictable character of the concrete. Tadao Ando calls it
the marble of the 20th century. He had already used it in Italy
a few years before at the Fabbrica de Benetton, with the same
construction teams. The thinners and the retarders must be
varied to ensure a homogeneous result, and the concrete's
execution requires precise planning before being poured into the
formwork. It was prepared on the mainland and brought over to
the building site in two huge containers carried on large barges,
before being pumped into the formwork.

To optimize the whole process, it was necessary to take the tides
and outside air temperature into account to ensure the
appropriate exothermic reaction of the poured concrete. At times,
the teams had to pour the concrete at five o'clock in the morning
or at nine o'clock in the evening. If the time required by the
retarders was exceeded, the concrete was poured elsewhere.
Moreover, no cast element was ever destroyed once it was
removed from the formwork and dried. This critical moment
required the entire team because so much of the architectural
project's success depended on it. M.D.

For Tadao Ando,
concrete is the marble
of the 20th century;
its imperfections testify
to its unpredictable
character.

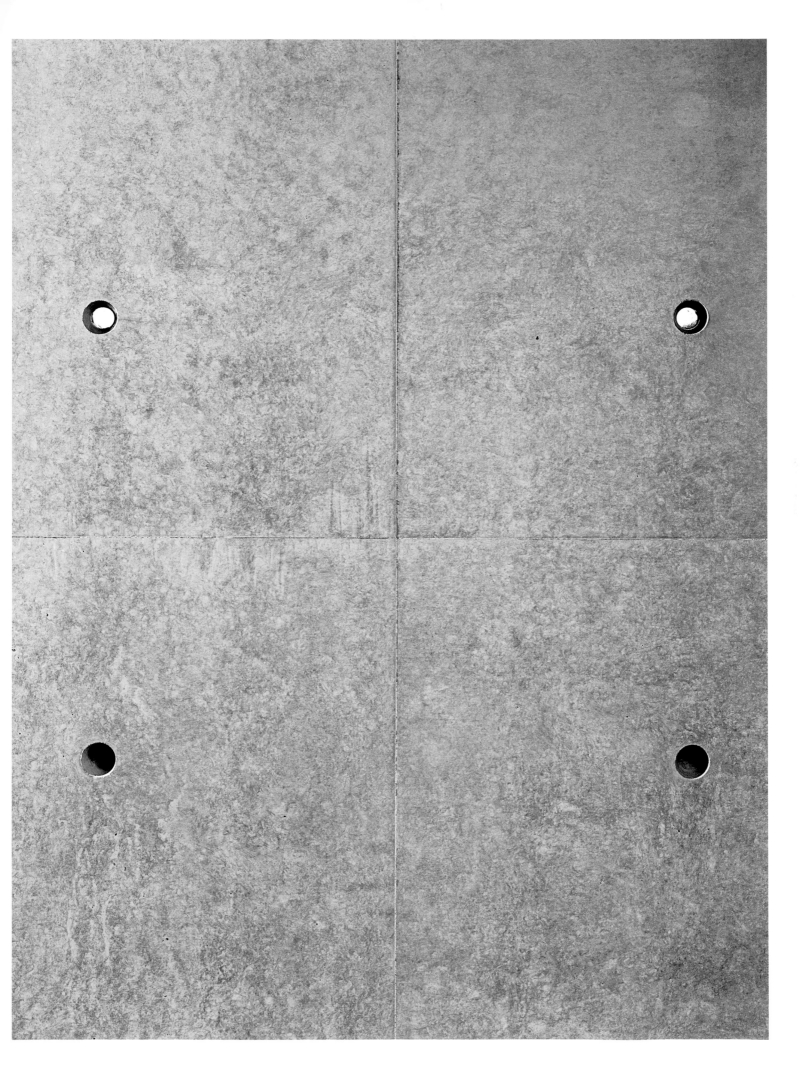

Alison Gingeras & Francesco Bonami, during the installation of Takashi Murakami's piece at Palazzo Grassi.

ALISON GINGERAS & FRANCESCO BONAMI

TWO CUTTING-EDGE CURATORS

Interview with Alison Gingeras and Francesco Bonami, by Fabrice Bousteau

40

FRANÇOIS PINAULT ENTRUSTED AN INTERNATIONAL DUET WITH THE TASK OF PUTTING TOGETHER HIS INAUGURAL MEGA-EXHIBITION. "MAPPING THE STUDIO" CREATES UNEXPECTED ENCOUNTERS BETWEEN ARTISTS FROM DIFFERENT GENERATIONS AND STYLES.

FABRICE BOUSTEAU: WHAT IS YOUR PERCEPTION OF TADAO ANDO'S PROJECT?

FRANCESCO BONAMI: It is magnificent and extremely subtle. He designed it to be entirely reversible and never made the slightest modification to the original building. His project, rather than challenging the past, adds to it and enhances it. In a certain sense, it is like the story of Romeo and Juliet: two lovers who are close without ever touching, the skin of two bodies that brush against each other and magnify each other.

Thanks to him, thanks to the artists, thanks to François Pinault, Punta della Dogana has become one of the rare buildings that brings together contemporary art, architecture (Tadao Ando) and the City of Venice.

HOW DID YOU GO ABOUT DESIGNING THIS EXHIBITION THAT YOU CALLED "MAPPING THE STUDIO"?

F. B. When we imagined the show, we began by observing the architecture of Punta della Dogana. At first I thought it was going to be **>**

"One has never seen such an unusual art center."

quite difficult because, in contemporary art, we are so used to the famous white cube and to artists complaining about how "the architecture is going to overwhelm the art." But little by little, we adjusted our sensibility, in particular by reflecting on what was done during the Renaissance, when paintings by the great masters were hung in churches and surrounded by golden frames, stained-glass windows, candles... without being diminished visually.

ALISON GINGERAS: And then there are all the parallels we did not anticipate and that were unveiled while we worked. When the Chapman brothers' work was installed, for example, a visual harmony, a basic geometry, immediately became apparent. So many of the things we had hoped for have come true in this place.

DO YOU MEAN TO SAY THE ARCHITECTURE PLAYED A FUNDAMENTAL ROLE IN THE EXHIBITION DESIGN?

F. B. We began by considering and analyzing the different kinds of spaces in the building because we had never seen such a huge center for contemporary art. We then concentrated on the "cube"—our unofficial name for the central gallery imagined by Tadao Ando—, to try to figure out what we were going to install in the symbolic heart of Punta della Dogana and the exhibition.

A. G. Using architectural drawings and a scale model of the building, we experimented with all the different combinations and tried several possible solutions. It has been a sort of game using the forms, the works of art, and the architecture. A puzzle as well. One work, placed in a particular space leads to another, and so on. And we came back to visit the building several times because only by seeing the space itself can you understand what must be done.

DID YOU DISCUSS IT WITH FRANÇOIS PINAULT?

A. G. He gave us complete freedom. When ideas came to us, we would discuss them with him because it is something he has a passionate interest in. He is very involved and loves to know how we are coming along, but he trusts us entirely.

F. B. We are often asked whether there are two curators or three, which is natural considering that the exhibition is based on a collection, with its own particular vision of contemporary art. Of course François Pinault played an important role in imagining this exhibition.

IN SEVERAL SPACES, WORKS BY YOUNG ARTISTS AND WELL-ESTABLISHED ARTISTS ARE DISPLAYED SIDE-BY-SIDE,

CREATING A SOMETIMES UNEXPECTED DIALOGUE BETWEEN THE TWO. ARE THESE CROSS-GENERATIONAL ENCOUNTERS ONE OF THE DRIVING FORCES BEHIND YOUR PROJECT?

F. B. From the start, we had the idea of contrasting generations, to avoid restricting ourselves to a succession of monographs. We then decided to "wed" well-established artists, like Twombly or Fischli & Weiss, to young artists who are still largely unknown, such as Richard Hughes or Mark Grotjahn. We played on this idea several times, here as well as at Palazzo Grassi.

A. G. This seemed all the more important to us because François is interested in different generations of artists, on the one hand, and also because he follows their careers over time. The way in which a work or an artist evolves fascinates him deeply.

IS THERE A PARTICULAR WORK IN THE EXHIBITION THAT HAS ICONIC STATUS?

A. G. When I designed the inaugural exhibition at Palazzo Grassi, "Where are we going?" it was the first time that the Pinault collection was being unveiled to the public. We therefore wanted to show its diversity and its breadth, with iconic images like Jeff Koons' *Balloon Dog*. The exhibition at Punta della Dogana will be semi-permanent, and we all—François Pinault especially—wanted to realize a project perfectly adapted to the space and capable of surprising, rather than one focusing simply on the "icons." This exhibition is truly the mirror of the singular approach François Pinault has adopted as a collector. I personally believe that Charles Ray's piece *Boy With Frog* will someday be an iconic image.

F. B. We began by thinking about the "essential" works and where they might be placed. Then, when we began taking into account the place itself, our reflection took a new turn, and the result is rather surprising. The building is like a mille-feuille pastry: all the ingredients are distinct, but when you take a bite, you savor all the flavors at once. From anywhere in the building, it is possible to discern original architecture and contemporary art, and all the while to be aware of, but not distracted by, the presence of the canal.

DESPITE THE IMMENSITY OF THE SPACES AND THE VARYING SIZES OF THE WORKS, THE BUILDING FEELS LIKE A HOUSE.

A. G. Most of the spaces are on a human scale. Only the first two halls are monumental, which is also a good thing. It forces us to work with new dimensions.

44

STILL LIFE AND TWIN TOWERS, BY TUYMANS

The great Belgian painter created this oversized *Still Life* barely a year after September 11, 2001.

What is the best way to depict an event such as this, that has been shown nonstop on television? By choosing to work within a traditional genre and with a peaceful image of a tray of fruits and a pitcher of water, Luc Tuymans anchors himself in an image of stability at the very moment when the world is overwhelmed with uncertainty. Nonetheless, the vast, endless white background lends a certain floating vulnerability to his subject, and its contours are hesitant. It is as if the artist were starting at zero. At Ground Zero.   JUDICAËL LAVRADOR.

"At Punta della Dogana, only the passage of time matters."

F. B. There was a process of natural selection. Over the past fifteen or twenty years, many artists have produced "spectacles," but what we are showing here cannot exactly be called "spectacular." Even if we wanted to organize a performance, the layout of the spaces makes it impossible.

A. G. It is about the relationship between the art and the spectator, about sensuality, about visualization. This building calls for an almost intimate connection with each piece of art presented.

IF YOU HAD TO ADVISE VISITORS, WOULD YOU TELL THEM TO START AT PUNTA DELLA DOGANA OR AT PALAZZO GRASSI?

F. B. It is the same story, told in two different ways, in two different places, with two different rhythms. Palazzo Grassi is a palace converted into a museum and belongs to the world. It is a more conventional place to hold an exhibition, and time is more "compressed." At Punta della Dogana, time has more substance; it lends itself to meditation and wandering.

A. G. I would begin the visit outside, with Charles Ray's statue *Boy with Frog*. It captures the story of Punta della Dogana, the place in Venice where people come for their first kiss or for their Sunday stroll. That explains why Venetians are so delighted with this opening. Then I would visit Punta della Dogana before crossing the canal to go to Palazzo Grassi.

ALISON, YOU ARE PROBABLY, ALONG WITH CAROLINE BOURGEOIS, THE PERSON WHO BEST KNOWS FRANÇOIS PINAULT'S COLLECTION. WHAT DOES IT SHOW? WHAT DOES IT REVEAL ABOUT HIS CONCEPTION OF ART AND LIFE? IS HE OBSESSED WITH THE IDEA OF DISCOVERING NEW FORMS OF ART AND MODES OF THINKING?

A. G. François Pinault has a very personal approach. For him, collecting art is not simply about accumulating the works of famous artists—that holds no interest for him. Art resides as much in Twombly's sublime abstraction as in a work as political as Paul McCarthy's *Train, Pig Island*. He loves constantly discovering new things, which is why he never tires of speaking with the artists and visiting their studios. Though it seems, at first, that he and the artists should be opposites in every way, each time there is a sort of magic connection created between the artist and the collector. François Pinault is especially interested and intrigued by their sensitivity, their intuition, their vision of society. What is inter-

esting is his choice to follow twenty artists. Not only is he loyal to them, but he also discerns what is new in their work. He tends to choose artists who evolve, who do not continually express the same message or produce the same works over and over.

YOU BOTH KNOW MANY ART ORGANIZATIONS THROUGHOUT THE WORLD—MUSEUMS, FOUNDATIONS, PRIVATE CENTERS... WHAT IS THE SPECIFICITY OF PUNTA DELLA DOGANA?

F. B. Punta della Dogana is the only place like it in the world, composed of different layers. You have to visit it because it is incomparable to anything in Florence, in Rome, or elsewhere... This building standing at the intersection of two large canals, visible from everywhere inside, brings together so many things. It features contemporary art, but it is not really or not only contemporary art that is on display, but rather contemporary art in this building and in this city.

A. G. More than a building it is an anchor. Imagine: beautifully restored 17th-century warehouses transformed into a contemporary art museum.

F. B. There is a space, in this building, that embodies the entirety: it is the room where Charles Ray's works are installed. If you look carefully, you can see Charles Ray's sculpture and, outside, along the canal, Palladio's church, the present and the past, all of history. I don't know whether Tadao Ando did it deliberately, but the experience of entering into Punta della Dogana is breathtaking: one moment you are on the Campo, in front of the Salute, and the next you are in what could be a Japanese interior! A few minutes is all it takes to feel completely isolated from Venice. Then, upon entering another room, Venice is suddenly present again.

A. G. It is such a theatrical experience of architecture.

WHERE ELSE IN VENICE WOULD YOU RECOMMEND GOING, FOR A VISITOR OF PUNTA DELLA DOGANA? WHAT IS YOUR FAVORITE PLACE?

F. B. Take the boat and go visit the little islands of the laguna. They are nameless, phantom places where the public boats do not stop.

A. G. Go to the Lido with a bicycle, then make your way to the end of the island and take the ferry that circles Pelestrina, the island closest to the Lido. Or the Frari, my favorite place. That's where Canova's heart is today. His hands are at the Accademia and his body in the little town of Bassano del Grappa.

MIKE KELLEY
Kandors Full Set
2005-2009,
21 bottles, hand
colored pyrex glass,
8 bottle stoppers,
10 silicone rubber,
8 urethane tinted,
6 plinths, veneer
Plexiglas and
lighting fixture,
21 tinted urethane
resin cities,
20 pedestals, MDF,
veneer, glass and
lighting fixture,
dimensions variable.

INAUGURAL EXHIBITION

Alison Gingeras & Francesco Bonami
(Excerpts from the exhibition catalogue "Mapping the Studio—Artists from the François Pinault Collection")

ENTITLED "MAPPING THE STUDIO", THIS EXHIBITION DERIVES ITS TITLE FROM A BRUCE NAUMAN VIDEO AND SEEKS TO RECREATE THE STEPS OF AN ARTWORK'S JOURNEY: FROM THE ARTIST'S STUDIO TO A PRIVATE COLLECTION TO THE PUBLIC EYE.

1/THE STUDIO, THE ARTIST, THE COLLECTOR

" The studio is a sacred territory. And for the artist, unlocking the door to that realm is a form of self-exposure that gives the outsider, even one who has been invited, a certain power. . . . The reciprocal confessional and critical dimension of the studio encounter forges a bond between the artist and curator. Concrete and symbolic transactions occur: the artist exchanges his or her vulnerability for access to the "system." Not only might an artist's work be included in an exhibition, but his or her practice stands to gain approval, to benefit from constructive critique or from broader art-historical contextualization. In return, the curator goes from stranger to confidant. The privilege of entry comes with responsibility—a curator cannot merely champion or utilize the artist's work without also sharing the frisson of the studio experience with a broader public. There is a moral imperative for the curator to somehow serve as a conduit between the intimate sphere of the artist and the outside world. Enter the collector. With the arrival of this new protagonist, the studio visit becomes an even more nerve-racking undertaking for all involved because it activates **>**

JEFF KOONS
Backyard
2002, oil-based jet on
canvas, 428 x 732 cm.

a new dynamic between the desire of possession and the trauma of dispossession. While the privilege of visiting the studio allows the collector to become immersed in the artist's private universe and to gain greater understanding of the artist and the artist's work, the possibility of acquisition looms large. Here the collector inhabits a dual role of enabling patron who provides the material means for the artist's experimentation, and a divisive force that pries the author from his or her beloved creation. This process is both invigorating and painful for the artist. Like many other private spaces, the studio is destined for eventual infringement—one way or another, a public culture is generated out of such transgressions of the private sphere.

By entitling the present exhibition of artists from the François Pinault Collection "Mapping the Studio", we hope to conjure the steps of a transformative journey of the artwork from the artist's private sphere to the hands of the collector to the public, who encounters the art in the exhibition space. During this progression, the artwork remains the same, but the circumstances of how it is experienced change with the context."

52

2/*MAPPING THE STUDIO* BY BRUCE NAUMAN

With his deceptively simple yet deeply poetic video installation *Mapping the Studio* (2000), Bruce Nauman makes manifest, in filmic time and in space, the Duchampian concept of the studio as state of mind. Using an infrared surveillance camera to film his workspace at night over the course of several months, Nauman captured "the nocturnal activities of mice, moths, and other sundry creatures," writes the curator Lynne Cooke, that "offers a wryly elliptical take on the mundanities of daily studio activity, as replete with languor as with moments of visionary insight."

The blurry, greenish surveillance footage becomes an allegory for the artist's thought process. At various points in the video, the cat appears, struggling to catch the mice. This pursuit is perhaps analogous to the creative struggle at the heart of every artist's studio experience, whether that space is physical or mental.

No matter how repetitive or ineffectual its task, the artist, like the cat, is compelled to endlessly chase and pounce on its creative pursuits. The cat-and-mouse metaphor might also be applied to the act of collecting.

It can certainly be conceded that collecting art itself is a creative activity that is nourished by the connoisseurs' emotional bond to both the physical objects he acquires as well as by the intellectual stimulation provided by the artwork. Through these connections and the process of accumulation, the collector forges an individual vision of art that is driven by a passion to pursue. When the collector charts a course through the ever-changing and ultimately unknowable territory of the studio, it is in an attempt to track down the artist's very best ideas and creations. A. G. & F. B.

BRUCE NAUMAN
Mapping the Studio
2001, video. Dia center;

3/A SHORT TYPOLOGY OF CONTEMPORARY STUDIOS

An exhibition such as "Mapping the Studio" registers the infinite permutations and possibilities of the artist's private universe. Artists such as Rudolf Stingel, Martin Kippenberger, Glenn Brown, or Marlene Dumas often labor in solitude, Jeff Koons, Damien Hirst and Takashi Murakami have all pushed Andy Warhol's notion of production to new heights by mobilizing small armies of artist assistants to help in the production of their paintings and sculptures while furthering their "brands" across international borders. Appropriating former industrial warehouses in various derelict neighborhoods of Brooklyn, artists such as Matthew Day Jackson, Urs Fischer, Rob Pruitt and Piotr Uklanski have created busy workshops that fuse a vibrant social scene with ambitious artistic production. Maurizio Cattelan works in a virtual studio as he surfs the web looking for inspiration. A theatrical stage set can serve as studio for Kai Althoff or Mike Kelley. Mark Handforth toils in a locksmith's garage in Miami and Mark Grotjahn paints in an anonymous storefront studio in Los Angeles while Jake and Dinos Chapmans' workshop resembles a sinister toy store full of menacing characters. Sigmar Polke's secretive lair in Cologne is like an alchemist's laboratory. Richard Prince has commandeered a whole suburban village in upstate New York as his atelier, while Adel Abdessamed, Mark Bradford and David Hammons use the streets as their studio. Hiroshi Sugimoto's collection of curiosities, fossils, and other historical artifacts feeds his work in both concept and form, while Cindy Sherman utilizes an expansive make-up room and a closet full of costumes before creating her iconic photographs. In Austria, the young artist group Gelitin and Otto Muehl, the legendary Aktionist artist, have integrated their radical experiments in communal living into a central component of their art-making.   A. G. & F. B.

THE ARTISTS FROM FRANÇOIS PINAULT'S COLLECTION IN THE EXHIBITION

Adel Abdessemed, Kai Althoff, John Armleder, Michaël Borremans, Mark Bradford, Glenn Brown, Christopher Büchel, Daniel Buren, Maurizio Cattelan, Jake & Dinos Chapman, Matthew Day Jackson, Marlene Dumas, Erro, Urs Fischer, Fischli & Weiss, Dan Flavin, Lucio Fontana, Tom Friedman, Gelitin, Robert Gober, Felix Gonzalez-Torres, Mark Grotjahn, David Hammons, Mark Handforth, Rachel Harrison, Richard Hughes, Mike Kelley, Martin Kippenberger, Jeff Koons, Barbara Kruger, Yayoi Kusama, Francesco Lo Savio, Nate Lowman, Lee Lozano, Paul McCarthy, Otto Muehl, Takashi Murakami, Bruce Nauman, Cady Noland, Raymond Pettibon, Huang Yong Ping, Michelangelo Pistoletto, Sigmar Polke, Richard Prince, Pruitt Early, Rob Pruitt, Charles Ray, Martial Raysse, Wilhelm Sasnal, Thomas Schütte, Cindy Sherman, Rudolf Stingel, Hiroshi Sugimoto, Jean Tinguely, Luc Tuymans, Cy Twombly, Piotr Uklanski, Franz West, Rachel Whiteread.

CHARLES RAY
Boy with Frog
2009,
cast stainless steel
and acrylic polyurethane,
247 x 91 x 96.5 cm.

GUIDED TOUR
OF THE EXHIBITION

1/PUNTA DELLA DOGANA

THE EXHIBITION TAKES PLACE IN TWO PLACES, PUNTA DELLA DOGANA AND PALAZZO GRASSI.
THE EXHIBITION TOUR OFFERED AT PUNTA DELLA DOGANA IS PRESENTED IN ITS ENTIRETY P. 99.

EXTERIOR
CHARLES RAY, *BOY WITH FROG*

Commissioned by François Pinault and created by the artist especially for Punta della Dogana, this sculpture of a young boy looking at a frog he just caught in the lagoon emotionally symbolizes the new artistic future of this historic Venetian site. It silently interacts with the expanse of canals surrounding it and with the three white façades of Palladio's marvelous churches, situated on the islands of San Giorgio and Giudecca. The simple and innocent gesture of the boy not only evokes a confrontation with nature and his own coming-of-age, but also offers a metaphor for our own rediscovery of the history and art of Venice, which we experience vicariously through the innocent gaze of the young boy.

With this figure of a young boy holding a frog in his fist, Charles Ray offers a contemporary reinterpretation of the *David* (c. 1440) created by young Donatello, who stands in a sensual *contrapposto* position with his foot resting on the head of Goliath. The young boy's treasure may appear modest, but he conquered it and now possesses it as his own. This act of violence evolves into an act of discovery: he marvels, astounded, at his own power. In the figure of the young boy can be seen that of the artist, ecstatic as he contemplates his potentially limitless creativity. The frog suspended in midair, which can be interpreted as an allegory of the act of creating, embodies the artist's reward in return for obeying the basic impulse to continue making art, to persevere in the search for his "prey." This impulse, an inherent part of human nature born out a sense of self-preservation, has survived all of the crises of history. This new figure standing before the Punta della Dogana, the symbolic and geographic heart of the Venetian panorama, reminds us that the urge to create burns eternally, a flame of hope for humankind.   A. G. & F. B.

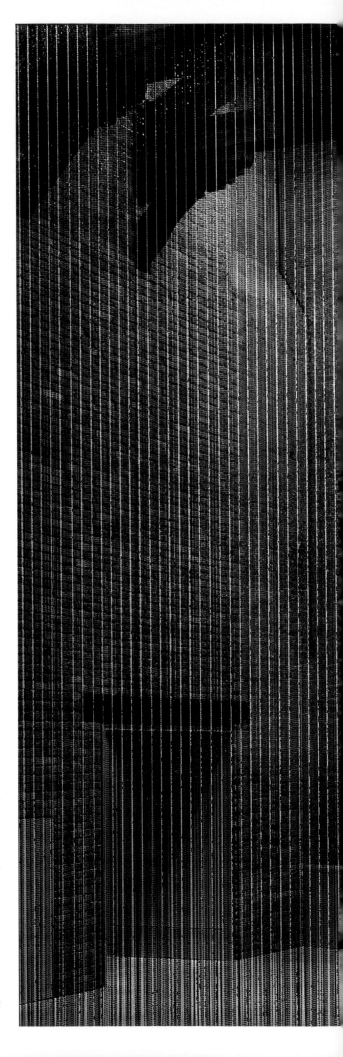

INTERIOR

A SELECTION OF EMBLEMATIC WORKS

NAVATA 1
FELIX GONZALEZ-TORRES *UNTITLED (BLOOD)*

The Cuban artist, who died from AIDS at the age of 39, left a body
of work that has become iconic in the art world, bittersweet pieces
that speak to universal communion and to the eternal solitude of
Being. Such a sentiment is made palpable with great sensitivity by
this curtain, *Untitled (Blood)*. While the red beads shine scarlet like
drops of blood, the white beads evoke the pills administered to the
sick. But the grace of the work resides in the form and function of
the curtain: fluid and volatile, it allows the spectator to pass. Two
sides, whose dividing line is not clearly marked: that of the sick,
always too far from the living, and that of the Others, us, you, me.
Each time we pass through, we experience both sides of the undu-
lating curtain. Created a year after the death of his companion, also
of AIDS, this work functions as a memorial, a minimal monument
that imbues itself with light from the space in which it is exhibited.
Here, through the curtain, one can perceive the mirrored image of
soul mates who have vanished.   J. L.

NAVATA 1
MAURIZIO CATTELAN *UNTITLED*

Like all of his works that use an animal as a
protagonist, Maurizio Cattelan's taxidermied
horse with its head stuck into the wall is an
allegory for the human condition. Reversing
the convention of an animal head as a hunting
trophy, Cattelan's horse has only its posterior
and body coming out of a wall. The viewer
cannot help but wonder if the horse's head is
protruding from the other side... Why would a
horse attempt to jump through the wall? This
absurd, tragicomic sculpture captures in a
single poignant image the struggle and toil of
our everyday lives.

Art-historically, the works makes a sly reference to a famous painting by Piero Longhi
(1701–1785). In much the same way that
Longhi, in his peculiar painting *The Rhinoceros*
(1751; in the Ca' Rezzonico collection), represented a group of high-society Venetians exa-
mining this exotic animal, Cattelan introduces
his horse into a "serious" artistic setting, both
as an element of surprise and as bitter com-
mentary on the craziness of society today.

A. G. & F. B.

62

2ND FLOOR – GALLERY 14
JAKE & DINOS CHAPMAN
FUCKING HELL

The grisly scene in the Venetian master Vittore Carpaccio's magnificent painting *The Ten Thousand Crucifixions on Mount Ararat* (1515), exhibited at the Gallerie dell'Accademia, narrates the terrible violence of the Roman army following their victory over the Armenian rebels. This work from nearly five hundred years ago prefigures the equally nightmarish vision of human barbarity in *Fucking Hell* (2008) by Dinos and Jake Chapman, which shows miniature sculptures of Nazi soldiers perpetrating their crimes against humanity.

The Chapman brothers' original *Fucking Hell* burned in a fire in London in 2000 and was remade identically. The nine glass "boxes" that comprise the work seem to have been made for Ando's architecture. The light, changing over the course of the day, acts as a projector of history, illuminating certain scenes of horror as if they were part of a film playing out before our eyes. A. G. & F. B.

ON THE WALL
CY TWOMBLY
Coronation of Sesostris 2000,
acrylic, pencil
and wax crayon
on canvas, ten panels,
dimensions variable.

ON THE GROUND
RICHARD HUGHES
Broken Circle
2006, polystyrene, wire,
jesmonite, stone powder,
epoxy resin, leaves, lacquer,
acrylic paint, three elements,
170 x 80 x 80 cm,
165 x 60 x 75 cm,
80 x 80 x 50 cm.

2ND FLOOR – GALLERY 13
CY TWOMBLY
AND RICHARD HUGHES

This set of surprisingly colorful paintings
by Cy Twombly takes on a new dimension
in Punta della Dogana. Like frescoes, the
panels seem almost to meld into the stone
walls, illuminating a sculpture in the center of the room by the young artist Richard
Hughes. The sculpture is deceptive: what
at first appear to be graffiti-covered rocks
from a park are in reality in the shape of
teeth, canines and a molar. Twombly and
Hughes have in common the power and
simplicity of their works, and their coming
together invites meditation.

SIGMAR POLKE
«Axial Age» series
2005, violet pigments,
mixed media on fabric,
six panels,
300 x 480 cm &
480 x 900 cm
(triptych).

66

FIRST FLOOR — GALLERY 2
SIGMAR POLKE

The monumental series "Axial Age" by the
influential German artist Sigmar Polke—six
panels and a triptych—was painted
between 2005 and 2007. The title is a reference to the term coined by Karl Jaspers
to describe the period between 800 BC and
200 BC, during which the world was rein-
vented based on the principle of transcen-
dence—a concept that finds full expression
in this series of paintings. Polke makes use
of a broad range of materials in his work,
including varnishes and pigments, photographic chemicals, gold and silver, lapis
lazuli and malachite—all references to
alchemistic processes of transformation.
Indeed, with these extensions of painterly
techniques, the artist undermines the picture itself, for any shift in perspective or
lighting is accompanied by a change in the
painting's appearance. The figurative elements are taken from 18th and 19th century engravings—such as from the tales of
Jules Verne and *Alice in Wonderland*.
A. G. & F. B.

HANGING

CINDY SHERMAN
Untitled
2007-2008,
six color photographs,
194.9 x 147.3 cm,
152.4 x 101.6 cm,
110.5 x 86.4 cm,
153.7 x 121.9 cm,
160 x 177.8 cm.

STANDING

JEFF KOONS
*Bourgeois Bust – Jeff
and Ilona*
1991, Carrara marble,
113 x 71.1 x 53.3 cm.

2ND FLOOR – GALLERY 10
CINDY SHERMAN
AND JEFF KOONS

Inspired from Antonio Canova's *Psyché Revived by The Kiss of Love*, Jeff Koons' *Bourgeois Bust*, showing the artist embracing his former wife, Ilona Staller, is one of the artist's iconic works. It acquires specific meaning at Punta della Dogana because Venice is the sculptor's home city, which contains the church housing his heart. The Carrara marble echoes with the white façade of the Palladio church, which the visitor can see beyond the piece, on the other side of the canal.

Cindy Sherman's portraits of women fashionably dressed, wearing a lot of makeup and trying to look younger than they really are, form a "masquerade" around Koon's piece, which reminds us of Venice and its carnival.   A. G. & F. B.

LEFT

RUDOLF STINGEL
Untitled
(Alpino 1976)
2006, oil on canvas,
335.9 x 326.4 cm.

RIGHT
Untitled,
2008, oil and enamel
on canvas,
three paintings,
330.2 x 487.7 cm each.

70

1ST FLOOR – GALLERY 3
CENTRAL COURTYARD
STINGEL

The central courtyard, comprised of
Ando's signature slabs of concrete poured
on site, is representative of his elegant
minimalist architecture. The architectural force of this space required from the
curators an adequate artistic response to
this aesthetic language. Working with
Rudolf Stingel, we chose four of his momu-
nental paintings—one for each wall: three
abstract works, covered with links of
chain forming the image of a cage, frame
Alpino (2007), a self-portrait of the artist
as a soldier realized in a photo-realistic
style. This monumental self-portrait has
an imposing presence in the gallery. It
echoes the astonishing use of scale in
Veronese's (1528–1588) art and recalls
his mannerist style that so astounded his
colleagues. 16th-century critics spoke of
the sensuality of Veronese's works, which
they described as "serenity almost perfectly suspended in a radiant calm"; this
description equally applies to the myste-
rious black-and-white of Stingel's self-
portrait. His works suffice unto themselves. It is art with a strong enough
presence to hold it own against the architecture without further embellishment
A. G. & F. B.

2ND FLOOR – GALLERY 9
CHARLES RAY

This gallery is composed almost as a succinct, small-scale retrospective, starting with one of Charles Ray's earliest works *Untitled (glass chair)*, 1976. For this deceptively simple work, Charles Ray cut an ordinary wooden kitchen chair in half, extracting 2 cm of wood, and replaced it with a sheet of glass. This minimalist gesture creates the appearance of a floating chair, and when installed at the Dogana with a view onto the Canal della Giudecca, the resonance with the watery landscape is astonishing.

This work is complimented by a recent sculpture, *Light from the Left* (2007), a bas-relief that represents the artist giving a flower to his wife on the day of their wedding. While the subject matter is rather prosaic, the artist makes a deliberate aesthetic reference to the bas-reliefs of ancient Assyria and Mesopotamia. This romantic work mesmerizes us with its seemless fusion of everyday reality and the persistance of the most ancient forms of artistic representation.   A. G. & F. B.

ON THE GROUND
MAURIZIO CATTELAN
All
2008,
white Carrara marble,
nine sculptures,
85 x 195 x 40 cm.

ON THE WALLS

HIROSHI SUGIMOTO
Series «Stylized
Sculpture»
2007,
twelve photographs,
gelatin silver prints,
149.2 x 119.4 cm.

2ND FLOOR – GALLERY 7
CATTELAN AND SUGIMOTO

The Carrara marble work of Cattelan is juxtaposed with
Hiroshi Sugimoto's new photographic series entitled
"Stylized Sculptures." These images of anonymous women
wearing iconic designers' clothes throughout the 20th century (Dior, Saint Laurent, Comme des Garcons, Cardin...)
were taken from the collection of the Metropolitan Museum
of Art's Costume Institute. This series extends Sugimoto's
work on the "history of history" in which his camera works to
highlight the museographic objects' formal qualities— line,
volume, color—over their historical content.   A. G. & F. B.

2ND FLOOR – GALLERY 12

FISCHLI & WEISS
ET MARK GROTJAHN

The enormous piece of wood sunken in
black rubber by Fischli & Weiss reso-
nates with the creations of Mark Grotjahn,
who toys with abstraction and with the
variation of surfaces according to natural light. His "butterfly" pictures, both
conceptual and sensual, conjure up sun-
sets, and their overlapping layers of
paint evoke, in keeping with Ryman, the
actual process of painting. .   A. G. & F. B.

PAUL MCCARTHY
Train, Pig Island
2007,
polyurethane foam,
mixed media,
266 x 558 x 124 cm.

OPPOSITE ON THE WALL
MARLENE DUMAS
Gelijkenis I & II
2002, oil on canvas,
two elements,
60.5 x 230 cm each.

ON THE GROUND
THOMAS SCHÜTTE
Efficiency Men
2005, steel and silicone,
pink: 230 x 55 x 120 cm,
green: 230 x 55 x 110 cm,
yellow: 230 x 55 x 119 cm.

1ST FLOOR – GALLERY 5B
THOMAS SCHÜTTE
ET MARLENE DUMAS

Thomas Schütte relates modern forms to expressionism, baroque, and mannerism. He derives no aesthetic pleasure from this historical and visual exercise but uses it instead as a means of forging a new language that is both dramatic and enigmatic. Shying clear of abstraction, he attempts to recover the universal dimension of sculpture, and its capacity to evoke the human experience.

Marlene Dumas, born in South Africa in 1953, explores existential themes – death, violence, sexuality – with a remarkable economy of means. Her clear, limpid painting, which confronts us with strange figures on a dark, obscure ground, is truly provocative.   J. L.

OPPOSITE ON THE WALL

ROBERT GOBER
Male and Female Genital Wallpaper
1989, hand printed silkscreen on paper, dimensions variable.

LEE LOZANO
No Title
c. 1963, crayon, graphite and collage on paper, eleven drawings, dimensions variable.

ON THE GROUND

ROBERT GOBER
Untitled
2006-2007, bronze and paint
63.5 x 119.3 x 182.8 cm.

82

1ST FLOOR – ROOM 4A

RICHARD PRINCE AND CADY NOLAND

Cady Noland belongs to a category of artists that has become too rare, one whose high standards are such that their work is a constant quest for perfection. Her work dissects the myths, ideals, and dreads underpinning American society since the 1960s. The cowboy is one of its most pregnant symbols, full of contradictions: a model of authenticity that has completely lost its marks, an honest but violent male, now become an advertising icon.

The black and white image drawn from the pages of a magazine showing an aged, toothless, gaping cowboy is certainly a way for the artist to kill the myth, but it is also a means of dressing it up to tear it down: the heavy earring may allude to the chains of black slaves, or to traditional Indian dress, or to S&M gear. In the end, Cady Noland demonstrates the power of the media image: outlined in the style of advertisements, this silkscreen simply leans against the wall, a sculpture devoid of a pedestal and a third dimension—a statue that walks upside down   J. L.

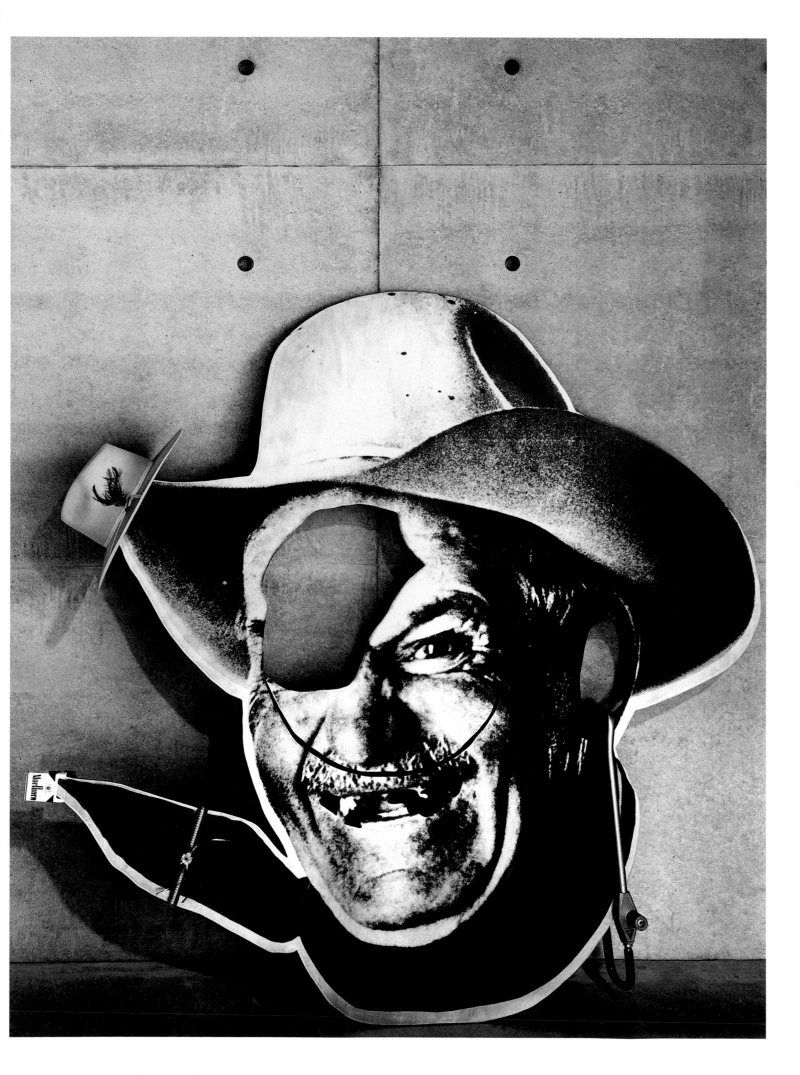

FISCHLI & WEISS

In the early 1980s, the Swiss artist duo Peter Fischli and David Weiss invented the characters of "Rat and Bear" as animal representatives for themselves. Before creating the work on display at the Dogana, Fischli & Weiss made the films *The Least Resistance* (1981) and *The Right Way* (1983) in which the artists, disguised as these two animals, parody both the art world and the wilderness. These two characters, Rat and Bear, are like modern day characters from the existentialist masterpiece *Waiting for Godot*—Vladimir and Estragon. For this new work, which takes the form of a mobile suspended from the wooden beam ceiling of the first floor of the Dogana's tower structure, the Rat and Bear float above our heads in space. Do they chase each other or are they simply wandering in a dreamy reverie? This work manages to amuse and astound the visitor, transforming this historical site within the Dogana into a cabinet of curiosity.

A. G. & F. B.

TOWER – 1ST FLOOR
MARK HANDFORTH

Mark Handforth—a young English artist based in Miami—was commissioned by François Pinault to create a special sculpture for this extremely unique space at the top of the ancient tower overlooking the Punta. Handforth who is already well represented in the Pinault Collection, decided to create an anthropormophized depiction of the moon. His *Man in the Moon* is suspended by a chain that links it to the famous sculpture of the *Fortuna* by Bernardo Falcone (c. 1677) that adorns the top of the Tower on the outside.   A. G. & F. B.

2/ PALAZZO GRASSI

Greeted by an amazing sculpture by Tinguely,
the visitor, as he enters the most intimate spaces
of Palazzo Grassi, is constantly taken aback
by the masterpieces before him. From French artist
Daniel Buren's iconic "variable forms" paintings
(1966), to a huge mural by Takashi Murakami—
commissioned by François Pinault and two years
in the making—, to the eighty Chapman Brothers
drawing inspired by Francisco de Goya...,
it is an invitation to embark on a unique journey
into contemporary art.

MARTIAL RAYSSE
Le Carnaval à Périgueux
1992,
tempera on canvas,
300 × 800 cm.

MARTIAL RAYSSE

Martial Raysse does not give interviews. During the cycle of conferences "Waiting for Punta della Dogana", he gave, on March 18, 2008, a few keys to understanding his vision of art.

"There is a first inspiration and a second inspiration. . . . The first inspiration has to do with someone who is in direct contact with the Heavens, the emotion reaches him directly... That's Ariosto, that's Dante; in France, it is someone like Rimbaud. Then, there is the second inspiration, that's Petrarch, for instance. It is the king that touches very educated people, great poets, like Mallarmé. . . . I am a poet, and I love Mallarmé. One of these critics/poets even told me I was 'post-mallarmean'. . . . When, during my first exhibition in Paris. . . . people told me, 'this is post-Poussin'. . . . I was exhilarated! It was meant to be a criticism, but I found it marvelous that people were finally able to see Poussin. . . . A work of art is like bottled intelligence, it makes its way through time, it is ageless, like the clouds. . . . The only thing that is truly important is to have a good understanding of 'what it tells.' When you see a painting, you must ask yourself. . . . 'Ultimately, what is this guy telling me, and what use is it going to be to me?' Everything else is pointless. A painting must speak; you must take the risk of speaking, you must take the risk of speaking through painting, you must deliver a message, you must fuel the arguments for a pure and sane vision of life!"

RICHARD PRINCE

Richard Prince, a hero of appropriationism —a typically American movement from the beginning of the 1980s—draws his inspiration from Willem de Kooning's famous *Women* paintings, showing nudes hyper-eroticized by the jittery brushwork of the pope of abstract expressionism. But Richard Prince goes a step further, adding photographs of porn actors and actresses that he then smears with paint. The brushstrokes both conceal and reveal these hermaphroditic figures. The confusion between the sexes is echoed in the confusion between different mediums: photography versus painting, as well as modern art versus images of mass media. The figures, engendered by these histori-cal and cultural splits, float on a black and purple canvas that appears both caver-nous and airy. The paintings are at once exhibitionist and introverted.   J. L.

PAUL McCARTHY

A Bear and a Rabbit, two adorable, larger-
than-life stuffed animals playfully frolick-
ing or, rather, doing you-know-what: this
animal (and unnatural) embrace captures
the essence—brilliant, salacious, fero-
cious, mocking—of the work of this late-
blooming artist. He is one of the best representatives of so-called "West Coast trash"
art, defined by its critical gaze that owes
much to both conceptual and pop art, used
by Los Angeles artists to dismantle the
infantilizing ideology of our entertainment
society. Paul McCarthy, who began with
performance art, often includes his sculptures in videos or installations featuring
Pinocchio, Heidi, and their little friends in
scabrous positions, smothered in ketchup
or chocolate cream. Dizzying, orgiastic,
grotesque, his pieces reveal the unnamed,
the violence of social conventions, and the
tyranny of normative representations in
contemporary society. Paul McCarthy
makes use of a scatological clownishness
that crosses *Ubu-Roi* with a Bettelheim-like
analysis of fairy tales, in the age of the
Disney Channel.   J. L.

ABOVE

ROB PRUIT
101 Art Ideas
You Can Do Yourself
1999, mixed media,
dimensions variable.

OPPOSITE

PAUL McCARTHY
Bear and Rabbit
on a Rock
1992, mascot heads,
acrylic fur,
metal armature,
foam rubber,
Formica pedestal,
270 × 190 × 130 cm.

94

TAKASHI MURAKAMI

"In relation to the rest of my body of work, this piece is the most important in my career because of its dimensions, and the time it took to design and realize. I conceived it as a tribute to François Pinault, who is one of the greatest collectors in the world and also the one who owns the greatest number of my works! It is a complex piece, a mural as well as a puzzle, that will require days and nights of close examination by François Pinault before he can understand all of its keys and meanings. There is, for instance, a wiseman, inspired from a Chinese legend, who invented agriculture and medicine. He eats grass. In this legend, if the grass is good for his health, his stomach lights up; in the other case, it blackens. The bowl flying over his head is a reference both to UFOs, very present in ancient Japanese art, and to another legend that tells of the rice collected from the rich and given to the poor. There is a lion-tiger, flower-hair... There are thousands of stories to discover."

INTERVIEW BY FABRICE BOUSTEAU

THE STORY OF PALAZZO GRASSI

Charles Poiré

THE WORLD-FAMOUS PALAZZO GRASSI, AN EMBLEMATIC PALACE OF VENICE, WHERE FIAT USED TO ORGANIZE MYTHICAL EXHIBITIONS, WAS BOUGHT BY FRANÇOIS PINAULT IN 2005 AND RENOVATED BY TADAO ANDO.

The design of the Palazzo is attributed to Giorgio Massari (1687–1766), who is also responsible for the Ca' Rezzonico across the Grand Canal. The Grassi family from Chioggia, at the far end of the Laguna, and from Bologna before that, had bought a parcel of land that provided for a large façade on the canal. The construction of the palace was most likely completed after the death of its patron in 1748, making it the last palace built in Venice before Napoleon overran the republic. In 1840, the Grassi heirs gave up the palace to a commercial business; thereafter, it went through a series of purchases and sales before a Greek financier implemented significant transformations in 1857: in the halls, he added four columns, and in the large first-floor ballroom he created an antechamber with rib vaults, known as the room of the *Triumph of Neptune and Amphitrite*. A new series of owners followed, until 1949, when a real estate company established a fashion museum in the palace. Subsequently, the courtyard was covered by a glass canopy, the garden was destroyed and replaced by an open-air theatre, and the old floor was covered with marble flagstones. Finally, in 1983, the palace passed into the hands of Fiat. Giovanni Agnelli,

l'Avvocato, commissioned renowned architects Gae Aulenti and Antonio Foscari to transform it into an exhibition center. The two associates installed paneling throughout that was placed at a distance from the walls, and that folded at the top to form 60 cm cornices. This transformation was completed by a system of metal plates equipped with spotlights. The work of the two architects ensured that the building would meet modern exhibition standards for a long time, in addition to the fact that they had completed their transformation with the installation of air-conditioning and new electricity and security systems.

TADAO ANDO'S RENOVATION

In 2005 Palazzo Grassi was purchased by the great modern and contemporary art collector, François Pinault, who asked renowned architect Tadao Ando to carry out a refitting of the palace. Tadao Ando has formidable experience designing museums. In particular, he is the creator of the Naoshima and Fort Worth museums. He knew François Pinault well because he won the competition to create an exhibition center for the French patron's collections at Île Seguin in 2001, before

the project was abandoned. From the outset, he decided to preserve the main spatial and architectural qualities of the building, including its geometrical irregularities, thus guaranteeing the principle of reversibility which is appropriate for a protected historic building. He developed a sober and minimalist style that let the exhibited works completely express themselves. Gae Aulenti's paneling was rectified.

"The neutral effect thus produced gives the impression of looking at a work by Donald Judd", the architect likes to comment. The marvelous 18th-century ceilings, with their decorated beams and their moldings, were preserved on the first floor, while those on the second floor were simply covered. The silhouette of the paneling, simple and stark, encircles the framework of the old doors; the staircases are covered with white *marmorino*, while the floors of the exhibition room are covered with white linoleum. Great attention was paid to the original materials of the Palazzo: thanks to the talent of local craftsmen who have preserved the secular traditions of "La Serenissima", it was possible to reconstruct certain elements in marble and Venetian stucco, in particular in the main staircase. 1,900 spotlights were ordered by the Danish artist

Olafur Eliasson from Ferrara-Palladino: they are retractable for each exhibition and integrated into extruded aluminum beams designed by Tadao Ando, and mounted on the walls so as not to damage the ceiling. The original structure of the glass canopy was restored and equipped with a coffered translucent shade. In five months, Tadao Ando completed his mission: to allow visitors to walk through simple spaces, suited to fluid movement from one room to the next, and to preserve the majestic beauty of the spaces without interfering with the straightforward exhibition of the works. The 40-room (5,000 m²) museum, directed by Jean-Jacques Aillagon, was inaugurated in April 2006 with the exhibition, "Where are we going?", under the direction of American curator Alison Gingeras. On the roster, the greatest artists of the last fifty years: Koons, Hirst, Rothko, Cattelan, Cindy Sherman...

Does this mean that the museum is exclusively dedicated to the exhibition of contemporary art? No. That is not the desire of its creator. Modern art exhibitions, as well as those from former great periods of history and civilization are also planned, like the 2008 exhibition "Rome and the barbarians".   •

Bibliography

«MAPPING THE STUDIO – ARTISTS FROM THE FRANÇOIS PINAULT COLLECTION»
under the direction of Francesco Bonami and Alison Gingeras. Catalogue of the exhibition of the works of the François Pinault Foundation at Punta della Dogana and Palazzo Grassi,
300 p., 250 ill., ed. Electa.
English, French and Italian editions.

THE CLIENT AND THE ARCHITECT – TADAO ANDO FOR FRANÇOIS PINAULT IN VENICE
under the direction of Francesco Dal Co
280 p., 230 ill., ed. Electa,
English, French and Italian editions.

ANDO, COMPLETE WORKS
Philip Jodidio
500 p., ed. Taschen, Cologne, 2006.
English and German editions.

General information

PUNTA DELLA DOGANA
Dorsoduro, 2
30123 Venezia
Vaporetto stop: Salute (line 1)
Tél. +39 041 523 16 80
Fax +39 041 528 62 18

PALAZZO GRASSI
Campo San Samuele, 3231
30124 Venezia
Vaporetto stops: San Samuele (line 2), Sant'Angelo (line 1)
Tél. +39 041 523 16 80
Fax +39 041 528 62 18
www.palazzograssi.it

Opening hours
«Mapping the Studio – Artists from the François Pinault Collection»
Opening June 6, 2009.
Open everyday from 10 am to 7 pm (last entrance 6 pm).
Closed every Tuesday. Closed on December 24, 25, 31, 2009 and January 1st, 2010.

The ticket for the 2 sites is valid for three days
– Full rate : 20 € for the visit of the two sites / 15 € for the visit of the one site.
– Discounted rate 1 : 17 € for the visit of the two sites / 12€ for the visit of the one site.
– Discounted rate 2 : 14 € for the visit of the two sites / 10 € for the visit of one site.
Every Wednesday, free entrance for Venetians (on presentation of an ID card or an IMOB card).

Réservations et préventes
Call center Vivaticket
www.vivaticket.it
By phone Monday to Friday from 8 am to 8 pm and Saturday from 8 am to 1 pm (paying call)
From Italy / 199 139 139
From abroad / +39 0445 230 313

PALAZZO GRASSI SHOP ET DOGANA SHOP
Situated on the first floor of Palazzo Grassi and Punta della Dogana, the bookshops are managed by the Italian publisher Electa, specialized in art and architecture publications.
In the premises, fully designed by Tadao Ando, you may purchase the various catalogues illustrating Palazzo Grassi and Punta della Dogana exhibitions as well as a wide range of art and architecture books and exclusive merchandising products.
Open from 9 am to 7 pm
Palazzo Grassi shop: +39 041 528 77 06

PALAZZO GRASSI CAFÉ
On the second floor of Palazzo Grassi, with a breathtaking view on the Grand Canal and Campo San Samuele, the Palazzo Grassi Café is managed by Irina Freguia, from the Venetian restaurant Vecio Fritolin and offers a large choice of venetian and Italian food.
Open from 10 am to 6.30 pm
Tel: + 39 041 24 01 337

DOGANA CAFÉ
Situated on the first floor of Punta della Dogana, Dogana Café is managed by Culto by Airest.
Open from 10 am to 6.30 pm.

A publication by
BEAUX ARTS ÉDITIONS / TTM ÉDITIONS
PRESIDENT Thierry Taittinger
EDITOR Claude Pommereau
PUBLICATION DIRECTOR
Fabrice Bousteau
ARTISTIC DIRECTOR Bernard Borel
SENIOR EDITOR
Séverine Cuzin-Schulte

PRODUCT MANAGER Laure Boutouyrie
SALES MANAGER Florence Hanappe
ASSISTANT PRODUCT MANAGER
Charlotte Ullmann

Beaux Arts éditions
86-88, rue Thiers
92100 Boulogne-Billancourt
Tél. +33 1 41 41 55 60 • Fax +33 1 41 41 98 35
www.beauxartsmagazine.com
RCS Paris B 435 355 896

EDITOR IN CHIEF Fabrice Bousteau
EDITOR Laurence Castany
GRAPHIC DESIGN Alice Andersen
PICTURE EDITOR Julie Le Borgne, assisted by François-Étienne Marchand
FRENCH EDITION COPY EDITORS
Malika Bauwens & Anne-Marie Valet
ENGLISH EDITION Robin Emlein & Michael Herrman
PROOFREADING Liz Ayre & Laure Boutouyrie
ITALIAN VERSION Elena Haddad
PROOFREADING Federica Mariat

SPECIAL THANKS TO : François Pinault, Tadao Ando, Jean-Jacques Aillagon, Alison Gingeras, Francesco Bonami, Renata Codello, Giandomenico Romanelli, Dominique Muller, Marc Desportes, Nazanine Ravaï, Eugenio Tranquilli, Monique Veaute, Marina Rotondo, Claudine Colin, Eva dalla Venezia, Anouk Aspisi, Verdiana della Penne, Delphine Trouillard, and in particular to all the artists from the François Pinault collection, as well as Alexandra Buffet, Florelle Guillaume and Élisabeth Barbay.

ISBN French version 978-2-84278-713-4
Italian v. 978-2-84278-715-8
English v. 978-2-84278-714-1
DÉPÔT LÉGAL June 2009
PHOTOENGRAVING Litho Art New, Turin
PRINTER Conti Tipocolor, Calenzano (FI)
[Printed in Italy].

BACK COVER
Point door of Punta della Dogana.